A Biblical Church Planting Manual

by Marlin Mull

Wipf & Stock
PUBLISHERS
Eugene, Oregon

Wipf and Stock Publishers
199 West 8th Avenue, Suite 3
Eugene, Oregon 97401

A Biblical Church Planting Manual
From the Book of Acts
By Mull, Marlin
Copyright©2000 by Mull, Marlin
ISBN: 1-59244-717-1
Publication date 5/25/2004
Previously published by The Wesleyan Church Corporation, 2000

TABLE OF CONTENT

CHURCH PLANTING

ACKNOWLEDGEMENTS

A number of people actively contributed to the current growing interest in new church planting. We owe an immense debt of gratitude to everyone that prays, gives and encourages this cooperative effort.

Patti Williams served as the graphic artist for this project, designing the cover and developing the illustrative materials.

Church planters, who dare to dream and then act on their vision for a new church, lead denominations. We cannot praise them enough for allowing God to use them for His glory and honor. Add to the list the spouses and children who sacrificially go to start a new church and reach lost people. Church planting families, your place in heaven has to be specially reserved. You are special!

Church planting is God's work. We acknowledge Him. He calls us. He goes with us. To Him alone should be the glory and the honor forever and forever. Amen.

PROLOGUE

Looking back, the new millenniums first breath of air concluded a previous century of movement faster than all of the previous centuries put together. Automobiles and airplanes moved us from place to place quicker than we would have imagined after the horse and buggy days of the nineteenth century. Outer space travel became a reality.

A world consciousness invaded our lives through radio, television, transistors and microchips. The Internet connected us instantly with those on line anywhere in the world. Medical discoveries almost eliminated polio and several other diseases. Today some people live because they carry other people's vital organs inside their bodies.

However, with all of the amazing discoveries listed above that offer possibility to enhance and prolong life, along with others, the Bible's evaluation of sinful humanity continues to be true. During the past century, man-induced violence, wars, death camps and famines spread like a terminal cancer as leaders and people want their own way, and no other way will do. The Atom and Hydrogen bombs hover over us to bring instant death to our enemies or us. Plagues like AIDS place all of us in physical peril.

In quick review, we can be apprehensive, discouraged or hopeful in this complex and confusing world. The principle answer to the world's problems and its hope for a successful life, now and in the future, lie in the Savior, Jesus Christ, and His church.

No one person can do everything to change this world. Yet, we can do what we can in our area of responsibility to present the good news of Jesus Christ through His church. That requires more churches.

The four gospels - Matthew, Mark, Luke and John- present Jesus Christ, God Himself, breaking into human history. Previously, there had been four hundred years of silence between the last book of the Old Testament, Malachi, and the first book of the New Testament, Matthew, when Jesus Christ arrived. He came – God lived on earth! Christ speaks as God to us directly, and we understand. He lives, suffers crucifixion and rises from the dead. The four gospels stir us, as we comprehend what Christ did for all of us personally. The foundation for the church comes into being.

The New Testament continues as Luke, almost without a pause, continues the story of Christ and the establishing of His church as a tool and force for righteousness in the Book of Acts, chapters one through twenty-eight. Most Bible translators title the Book the Acts of the Apostles. Some refer to it as the Acts of the Holy Spirit. **I believe an additional title for consideration could be the Bible's Church Planting Manual.**

My prayer is that Christ's church everywhere will live in Acts chapter twenty-nine (today) as a continuation of what is recorded in the Book of Acts, and based on it. The story of Jesus and the early church should not end. Jesus Christ laid the foundation for the church through His life, death and resurrection as recorded in the four gospels, Matthew, Mark, Luke and John. The followers of Jesus Christ then continued His work by spreading the gospel through preaching and teaching and the planting of new churches, as recorded in chapters one through twenty-eight in the Book of Acts.

What will it take to make a decision for planting new churches? Passion! If our motivation is to win people to Jesus Christ, we will respond with a passion for new church planting.

Today and tomorrow, we live in Acts chapter twenty-nine (my firm belief). To continue the work begun by Christ and His disciples, new church planting should be at the top of our list of priorities, as it was in theirs.

INTRODUCTION
"BOSS MAN, I'M A CHURCHMAN"

Those words sounded in my ears and more importantly in my heart when I first heard them. Some events bring about change in our lives. Other events reinforce and nurture our basic beliefs. Those words, "Boss man, I'm a churchman," strengthened my personal convictions about my own Christian experience.

Let me share about an interesting Christian. My shoes needed shining (not an unusual occurrence) after a long day of meetings and travel. Having time between planes in the Detroit airport, I wondered if any shoeshine stand would be open before the last flight left for Indianapolis at 11:00 p.m.

Then I saw a shoeshine stand. An elderly gentleman sat in a chair beside it leaning back against the wall. The downward tilt of his head suggested inactivity. He was ready for business, but taking it easy until a customer came.

"How about a shoeshine," I softly asked, waking him up.

"Sure thing, boss man," he replied with a sleepy smile.

After taking a seat on the stand, he noticed the book in my hand. It had a religious title. Then he started talking while I listened. I wrote part of his story on a blank page in the book.

"Boss man, are you a preacher?" he said in a tone louder than medium, but with a gentleness of manner.

"Yes sir," I answered him.

He continued, "Where do you preach?"

"Well, I preach a lot of places since I work out of a

9

denomination's international center in Indianapolis, Indiana. I relate to a number of churches."

"You do. Well let me tell you something boss man, I'm a churchman. I believe in the church. I have served the Lord for over fifty years. And I raised my children in the church."

I then asked him to tell me about himself, his children and the church.

Forrest now retired and originally from Georgia, worked for Delta Airlines in a maintenance crew at the Atlanta Airport until transferred to Detroit a number of years ago. He and his wife had, and raised, twelve children. To provide additional support for his family, he also shined shoes in the airport after getting off his regular job with the airline.

Several times while he briefly told me his life story, he repeated the phrase, "Boss man, I'm a churchman." His story verified his statement.

Forrest attends a church in the inner city where his brother is the pastor, and has been over thirty years. He made sure his children went to church. Proudly he related to me how his children had never been in trouble with drugs, gangs or other major teenage problems because he kept them in Sunday school and church.

Every one of his twelve children graduated from college. He named a number of well-known colleges and universities like Michigan State and the University of Michigan that they attended. His eight sons and four daughters have taken places of leadership in education, medicine and business. Forrest, now 73 and a widower, was rightly proud of his family. He should be. This Christian African-American worked hard. Today he shines shoes as something to do and a way to meet people. However, he attributed the success of his family to Christ and the church.

"Boss man, I'm a churchman."

Those of you taking the time to read this book can testify along with Forrest and me how much the church means to you and your family.

What thoughts do you have when the word "church" comes to mind?

If you grew up in a rural setting, you might envision a frame building with some splintered pews which seats about a hundred people when filled to capacity. A piano might provide the main source of music along with soft cover gospel songbooks.

Childhood memories may make their way through your mind. You remember when you squirmed through sermons, or crawled through basement windows during the Sunday school lessons while your teacher shared a stirring story from the Bible with a spiritual application. You listened, but the teachers wondered if they got through to the spirit in your active mind and body.

Do you remember that home church of yours where sacred moments took place that made major changes in your life? You said your marriage vows; dedicated your children to the Lord; brought your loved ones for final farewell words before taking their body out for burial; and went forward to the altar to pray for forgiveness, or to make new commitments and renew old ones.

Moreover, do you remember a special Sunday at your church when you felt you were alone before God as the preacher spoke for God directly to your soul? Then you said, "yes" to God's will and way for your life.

The word "church" can call up positive thoughts of joy, reverence, awe, inspiration, faith, saints past and present and lots of Christian love. I pray as you remember your church that it brings to mind meaningful memories.

Some (you) might express negative feelings of confusion, anger, rejection and disappointment when you think of a painful experience with a particular church. Too often people have been discouraged with the earthly church. Moreover, in some incidents they might have good reasons. People in the church disappointed us, when we thought they should have been there for our needs.

Yet without unfairly judging those with negative feelings about a particular church they have been a part of, let me remind you we often think negatively about the church as "them" not "I." With a negative mind set, unless we are prayerfully careful, the church can stand as a body or a group separate and distinct, apart from us.

We cannot forget the church is you and I. A personal, private faith in Christ begins the Christian life. However, to be whole, we need others called the "church." They complete our faith as we complete theirs. The church at its best represents the body of Christ.

"Boss man, I'm a churchman."

Everyone personally needs a church. This hurting and confused world needs the church. It needs more churches.

Some of you may be wondering about one important item. I did pay Forrest for the shoeshine and tipped him. He made a difference by verifying once again how important the church is in my life. I will look for the "churchman" the next time I go through the Detroit Airport. He enriched my life.

I am a churchman like Forrest. Everyone should have an opportunity to experience the love and privilege of serving and following Jesus Christ through a local church.

Before I begin in more detail, let me share with you the basic premise for this writing.

CHURCH PLANTING IS THE NUMBER ONE METHOD OF EVANGELISM!

Evangelism of the lost, those without Jesus Christ as a personal Savior, who might be more readily saved because a new church is planted, validate the need for this effort.

<u>Evangelistic Churches in North America</u>

In 1900, at the start of the previous century, 27 churches existed for every 10,000 people.

In 1950 at the middle of the previous century, 17 churches existed for every 10,000 people.

In 2000, at the beginning of this current new century, 11 churches exist for every 10,000 people.

12

WE NEED TO PLANT MORE CHURCHES

My prayer for this writing effort is that God will use it as another tool to awaken and challenge You, to be active in the planting of new churches. Since 1986, after my last pastorate, my family has been members of four different new church plants. I presently attend and my wife and I are charter members of the Fall Creek Wesleyan Church in Fishers, Indiana. It is a new church plant.

THE CHURCH AND THE BOOK OF ACTS

Many approaches can be taken to communicate my passion for everyone being involved in new church planting. Human reasons abound with solid evidence to back these approaches. However, my attempt will confine itself to the New Testament Book of Acts. Using the Book of Acts as a primary guide for our considerations hopefully will give biblical authority to what I want to share. Unless otherwise indicated, Scripture references are taken from the New International Version of the Bible.

I pray that my interpretations of the Scriptures will be valid and honoring to God's Word. If someone reads this presentation on church planting and feels that I have wandered too far astray, my intentions were not to use proof texts, but to let the underlying principles and direct teachings of the Bible convey the intended truth.

The Book of Acts uses the word *church* eighteen times and the word *brothers* several times clearly referencing the church. The following passages relate more directly to this effort.

After the stoning of Stephen, "On that day a great persecution broke out against the **church** at Jerusalem, and all except the apostles were scattered throughout Judea and Samaria" (Acts 8:1). Opposition forced the new church to expand beyond its comfort zone. Because of the persecution, new churches came into being. How do we know this? Read the following verses that relate to the subject of new churches.

"Then the **church** throughout Judea, Galilee and Samaria enjoyed a time of peace. It was strengthened; and encouraged by the Holy Spirit, it grew in numbers, living in the fear of the Lord" (Acts 9:31).

Peter receives a vision from the Lord to go to Cornelius's house. He goes with a representation from the Joppa church. "Then Peter invited the men into the house to be his guests. The next day Peter started out with them, and some of the **brothers** from Joppa went along" (Acts 10:23).

"The apostles and the **brothers** throughout Judea heard that the Gentiles also had received the word of God" (Acts 11:1). "The disciples, each according to his ability, decided to provide help for the **brothers** living in Judea" (Acts 11:29).

The word *Christian* first appears in the Bible in connection with the new church at Antioch. "Then Barnabas went to Tarsus to look for Saul, and when he found him, he brought him to Antioch. So for a whole year Barnabas and Saul met with the **church** and taught great numbers of people. The disciples were called Christians first at Antioch" (Acts 11:25-26).

The two church-planting pastors preached at Derbe, Lystra, Iconium and Antioch. Then, "Paul and Barnabas appointed elders for them in each **church** and, with prayer and fasting, committed them to the Lord, in whom they had put their trust" (Acts 14:23).

An authority resides with the church. "The **church** [Antioch] sent them on their way, and as they traveled through Phoenicia and Samaria, they told how the Gentiles had been converted. This news made all the **brothers** very glad" (Acts 15:3).

"Some time later Paul said to Barnabas, 'Let us go back and visit the **brothers** in all the towns where we preached the word of the Lord and see how they are doing'" (Acts 15:36).

Timothy a young preacher received a recommendation from two churches for ministry. "The **brothers** at Lystra and Iconium spoke well of him" (Acts 16:2).

The Ephesian **brothers** encouraged Apollos in his ministry (Acts 18:27).

In addition, the word **disciple** is used 28 times in the Book of Acts and can be used as a reference guide to the spread of the early church.

16

"When he [Paul] landed in Caesarea, he went up and greeted the **church** and then went down to Antioch" (Acts 18:22).

"From Miletus, Paul sent to Ephesus for the elders of the **church**" (Acts 20:17).

The Apostle Paul gives his farewell address to the Ephesian elders. He first reminds them of his credentials and faithfulness. Then Paul begins his instructions. "Keep watch over yourselves and all the flock of which the Holy Spirit has made you overseers. Be shepherds of the **church** of God, which he bought with His own blood" (Acts 20:28).

At Thessalonica, the church is composed of Jason and some other **brothers** (Acts 17:6). "As soon as it was night, the **brothers** sent Paul and Silas away to Berea" (Acts 17:10). At Berea, the **brothers** rescued Paul from the crowds (Acts 17:14). At Corinth, Paul left the **brothers** (Acts 18:18). Paul greeted the **brothers** at Ptolemais (Acts 21:7). He called the church **brothers** at Puteohi (Acts 28:14) and at Rome (Acts 28:15).

Chapter one of the Book of Acts concludes the personal, visible ministry of Jesus Christ on earth. Chapter two explodes with the day of Pentecost taking center stage. Read Acts chapter two again. Note the named areas of the then known world represented by people in Jerusalem who heard Simon Peter's sermon launching the church. As you read the rest of the Book of Acts, Simon Peter, Paul, Luke, Silas and Timothy plant new churches as they encounter people who were at Pentecost and heard Simon Peter preach. I believe Pentecost planted the initial seed for church planting in many areas of the world.

The Lord, through the Holy Spirit, started the church planting movement at Pentecost. It encourages me to realize that when the Lord prompts us to new church planting, He has already prepared the way.

TWELVE BIBLICAL REASONS
FOR STARTING A NEW CHURCH FROM
THE BOOK OF ACTS

1. A new church brings the Kingdom of God to earth (Acts 1:3; 8:12; 14:22; 19:8; 20:25; 28:23; 28:31).

2. A new church helps fulfill the Great Commission (Acts 1:8; Matt. 28:18-20; Mark 16:15-16; Luke 24:46-49; John 20:19-22).

3. A new church provides a place of prayer to meet God with others (Acts 1:14; 4:31; 12:5).

4. A new church provides another public preaching place (Acts 9:20; 10:42; 14:7; 16:10; 20:20).

5. A new church is the most effective evangelistic tool (Acts 2:38-39; 14:21).

6. A new church teaches the Bible (Acts 4:2; 5:19-21; 5:42; 8:4; 11:25-26; 18:11; 20:20; 28:31).

7. A new church offers another place for Christian service (Acts 6:3; 9:36; 11:25-26; 11:29-30; 17:15).

8. A new church trains lay leaders to become preachers (Acts 6:10; 14:23).

9. A new church crosses cultural barriers (Acts 8:35; 10:1-48; 16:9; 22:21).

10. A new church mentors new believers (Acts 9:26-28; 20:20; 20:31, 36; 20:34-36; 20:27).

11. A new church supports worldwide missionary activity (Acts 13:2-3; 16:9-10).

12. A new church starts other churches (Acts 13:2-3; 16:9-10).

TWELVE BIBLICAL REASONS FOR STARTING A NEW CHURCH FROM THE BOOK OF ACTS

ONE – A NEW CHURCH BRINGS THE KINGDOM OF GOD TO EARTH (Acts 1:3; 8:12; 14:21b-22; 19:8; 20:25; 28:23; 28:31)

The church emerges in the Book of Acts as God's instrument to reach the world with the good news. The Book of Acts can be outlined in several ways.

If you focus on persons, the first twelve chapters find their center on Simon Peter's ministry. The remaining chapters, thirteen through twenty-eight, relate to the Apostle Paul.

Most believe (as I do) that the basic biblical outline for the Book of Acts is found in 1:8 when Jesus said, "But you will receive power when the Holy Spirit comes on you, and you will be my witnesses in . . . "

Jerusalem (chapters 1-7),

and in Judea and Samaria (chapters 8-12),

and to the ends of the earth (chapters 13-28).

Note: At the beginning of each section, the kingdom of God is emphasized.

Jerusalem (Acts chapters 1-7)

"After his [Jesus] suffering, He showed himself to these men and gave many convincing proofs that he was alive. He appeared to them over a period of forty days and spoke about **the kingdom of God**" (Acts 1:3).

Jesus Christ's words laid the foundation for the beginning of the church in Jerusalem.

Judea and Samaria (Acts chapters 8-12)

"But when they [Samaria] believed Philip as he preached the good news of **the kingdom of God** and the name of Jesus Christ, they were baptized, both men and women" (Acts 8:12).

The Ends of the Earth (Acts chapters 13-28)

"Then they returned to Lystra, Iconium and Antioch, strengthening the disciples and encouraging them to remain true to the faith. We must go through many hardships to enter **the kingdom of God**, . . . " (Acts 14:21b-22).

"Paul entered the synagogue [Ephesus] and spoke boldly there for three months, arguing persuasively about **the kingdom of God**" (Acts 19:8).

"Now I know that none of you [Ephesians] among whom I have gone about **preaching the kingdom** will ever see me again" (Acts 20:25).

The Apostle Paul reaches Rome. "They arranged to meet Paul on a certain day, and came in even larger numbers to the place where he was staying. From morning till evening he explained and declared to them **the kingdom of God** and tried to convince them about Jesus from the Law of Moses and from the Prophets" (Acts 28:23).

The Book of Acts **begins** with Jesus teaching His disciples for forty days about the kingdom of God (Acts 1:3). It **concludes** with the last verse of the book telling of Paul's ministry. "Boldly and without hindrance **he preached the kingdom of God** and taught about the Lord Jesus Christ" (Acts 28:31).

From the beginning to the end, in the Book of Acts, the kingdom of God stands as a central theme and all that the term embodies. The kingdom of God arrives as a presence and force in this world through the church.

When we pray as Jesus taught His disciples to pray, and say, "Thy kingdom come" (Matt. 6:10 KJV), we pray at that moment for the church planting movement. To be a part of God's kingdom encompasses new churches. We have to give ourselves wholeheartedly to being involved in new church planting. If we have no interest in Kingdom building through new church planting, can we sincerely keep the words in our spiritual vocabulary, "Thy kingdom come"?

We confront a daily challenge. Is Kingdom building just for our benefit, or for all the people? God calls us as ministers, pastors and church leaders to do His work. Building His Kingdom means new church planting with all of our spiritual hearts, souls, minds and bodies.

TWO - A NEW CHURCH HELPS FULFILL THE GREAT COMMISSION (Acts 1:8; Matt. 28:18-20; Mark 16:15-16; Luke 24:46-49; John 20:19-22)

GREAT COMMISSION PARALLEL PASSAGES

	POWER	PURPOSE	PRESENCE
Matthew 28	All authority in heaven and on earth has been given to me (18).	Therefore go and make disciples of all nations, baptizing them in the name of the Father and of the Son and of the Holy Spirit, and teaching them to obey everything (19, 20).	And surely I am with you always, to the very end of the age (20).
Mark 16	The testimony of the resurrection. (9).	Go into all the world and preach the good news to all creation (15).	Whoever believes and is baptized will be saved, but whoever does not believe will be condemned (16).
Luke 24	This is what is written: The Christ will suffer and rise from the dead on the third day (46).	and repentance and forgiveness of sins will be preached in his name to all nations, beginning at Jerusalem (47).	I am going to send you what my Father has promised; but stay in the city until you have been clothed with power from on high (49).
John 20	Peace be with you! After he said this, he showed them his hands and side. The disciples were overjoyed when they saw the Lord. (19-20)	As the father has sent me, I am sending you. (21)	Receive the Holy Spirit. (22)
Acts 1	He showed himself to these men and gave many convincing proofs that he was alive (3).	You will be my witnesses in Jerusalem, and in all Judea and Samaria, and to the ends of the earth (8).	You will be baptized with the Holy Spirit (5). You will receive power when the Holy Spirit comes on you (8).

The range of the Great Commission reaches farther than we think. To better understand the Book of Acts we take chapter 1:8 and divide it into three geographical parts based on where we live. If you lived in Japan, all of the following would be adjusted to fit that geography. This is a North American viewpoint of Acts 1:8.

    a. Jerusalem (local) – This represents our local community responsibility.

    b. Judea and Samaria (North America) – This denotes our broader area of responsibility. It includes communities, towns and cities that connect with our community directly or in a closer geographical area.

    c. Ends of the earth (outside North America) – This corresponds to outreach beyond an easier connecting area.

Every pastor and congregation usually has a strong interest in reaching their local "Jerusalem" with the gospel. The very ongoing life of the local church demands and requires it. When this vision ceases, the church loses its effectiveness for ministry and eventually closes.

In addition, churches realize that to have a strong local church there needs to be an equally strong mission emphasis. Mission-minded churches thrive. However, how do you or I define missions?

Churches can emphasize in their preaching, teaching and giving, local needs (Jerusalem) and needs outside of North America (ends of the earth), while omitting North America (Judea and Samaria) as an important mission focus. Equally, North America belongs in a mission vision for reaching the lost.

Church planting is biblical and is the heart of the Great Commission. The apostles emphasized it. Church planting exalts Christ. It crosses all cultural barriers and continues to be the best method under heaven to effectively advance the gospel. New church planting breaks spiritual ground, expands the kingdom of God and rejuvenates denominations like no other way.

Too often, reaching the lost has been replaced by being afraid of losing the reached.

Planning the year's activity, as a pastor, for the local church is easy. Usually, we do the same things every year that we did in the preceding year. It might be a different speaker for those yearly special occasions, but the format remains constant. We plan activities to serve the existing congregation.

Church planting moves us out of comfortable routines and ruffles tradition. We need to be a part of fulfilling the commission given in the Bible by Jesus Christ to His church. That will shake us. Reaching the lost should drive us first, while at the same time we serve our congregation. Where does your church fit into the picture?

THREE - A NEW CHURCH PROVIDES A PLACE OF PRAYER TO MEET GOD WITH OTHERS (Acts 1:14; 4:31; 12:5)

"They all joined **together** constantly in **prayer**, along with the women and Mary the mother of Jesus, and with His brothers" (Acts 1:14).

"After they **prayed**, the place where they were meeting was shaken. And they were all filled with the Holy Spirit and spoke the word of God boldly" (Acts 4:31).

"So Peter was kept in prison, but the church was earnestly **praying** to God for him" (Acts 12:5).

The hundred and twenty believers met for prayer in the Upper Room just before the Day of Pentecost. A church founded on the sacrificial death and resurrection of Jesus Christ would spring forth in a few days. They wanted God's will. The next step in their lives needed to be God-ordered. Therefore, they met and prayed. Prayer brings unity. When church people pray together, it enables them to manage opportunities or difficulties with less tension.

We often think of church with personal memories of our home church, a first pastorate (for me), or other pleasant spiritual experiences. A need exists to also think of a new church as another house of prayer. Through the prayers of a new congregation, people in their immediate area of responsibility find Christ as Savior, experience positive changes, develop spiritual homes and new spiritual leaders emerge.

26

Personally, some of the most enriching times in my spiritual walk with the Lord have been experienced at the church altar while praying. Obviously, we can pray anytime and anywhere, and we should. Yet, something unique remains, at least for me, in the privilege to kneel at a church altar.

A new church can provide another place of prayer in general and a particular place of prayer at the altar for believers. As new converts won to Jesus Christ by a new church grow in the knowledge and wisdom of the Lord, they become prayer intercessors. A need always exists for people who pray. A new church provides additional opportunities for disciplining people who will pray.

New churches have to pray. Am I suggesting that established churches do not have to pray? No! I am suggesting that some established churches can subtly succumb to prayerlessness because of their financial resources and numerical strength. That dependence can be fatal. The Laodicean Church in Revelation 3:17 had the same attitude. New churches have to pray for God's help to begin and continue.

Questions of self-examination every pastor and church leader of established churches could ask themselves are these:

"Does my church unite in prayer as it did in its early beginning?"

"Do we depend more on our visible resources, people and finances, than our most valuable resource – God?"

New congregations, if properly begun, start out as a people joined in prayer. The people gathered in the Upper Room had been with Jesus. They saw Jesus perform miracles. They heard Him teach wonderful truths. They winced when He uttered words of judgment. They knew His gentle nature with sinners and children. Their first discipleship phase of training ends. What is next?

They pray, as any new church should, for God's guidance. A joy of serving in this office is the reports of new church plants and how they prayed through impossible situations. Land was needed. Finances were needed. A place to meet was needed. An obstacle threatened their existence. They prayed. God answered prayer.

When difficulties came, they prayed. After the early church heard the threats of the rulers, elders and teachers of the law in Jerusalem, they prayed. "After they **prayed**, the place where they were meeting was shaken. And they were all filled with the Holy Spirit and spoke the word of God boldly" (Acts 4:31).

This recent new church plant illustrates the power of prayer. Their launch day was May 7, 2000. The following letter was received from the pastor's wife.

Hi Friends,

I am writing to many of you who know us and who have been praying for our new church plant. We had our first service yesterday. What a day. I need to tell you an amazing story of how God provides.

On Saturday night, the eve of our first service, George and I, along with his brother and his wife, sat down around 7:15 p.m. for a meal. All was ready for the next day's service. All the "I's" were dotted, all the "t's" were crossed, and we had **prayed, prayed,** and **prayed** some more!

The phone rang. It was the banquet manager from the hotel where our first service would be held. The manager told George, "I have some bad news. We have double booked your room, and now we have nowhere for you to meet." We had been scheduled for a room that seated 125, with an adjacent room for children. We had signed our one-year lease contract in January. Needless to say, after spending close to $1,000 on newspaper and radio advertising, we were not very happy.

George was stunned as the guy began to ask if we could move our first service to the next week, or if we could move to another hotel, both of which

28

were impossible. George hung up the phone hoping the other group that was supposed to be in the room would agree to move. They didn't.

We immediately began to **pray,** and called others to **pray** that God would make a way. The situation seemed bad, but we knew God was in it. We just weren't sure what He was going to do.

The manager didn't have a bad attitude. It was an honest mistake. None-the-less, we were still out of the room. We called him back with an alternate suggestion. He said he couldn't do it. George went to the hotel, hoping and **praying** to negotiate something.

When George arrived, the banquet manager, Troy, a very professional capable man, whose father was a pastor, and who knew what this service meant, was in tears, apologizing profusely for the mistake. George reassured him that everything would be okay and **prayed** with him. In a short period of time, we agreed to meet outside.

Here is the miracle.

(1) The seating outside was beside the pool area, under a beautiful tent with seating for 150. It was a gorgeous day.

(2) At our service, we had 153 people. We could NEVER have fit everyone into the other room, which seated only 125.

(3) Because of the mistake, Troy agreed to give us RENT FREE, the ballroom, which is four beautiful rooms put together. Three of the rooms seated 650 with a room left over for the children. He is giving us these rooms, rent free, for ONE YEAR. These rooms rent for $450 per week. That totals to around $21,000 free rent. It truly is a miracle.

(4) Out of the 153 that attended our first service, some came just for moral

support for our first service (family, friends). If we leave these people out, we had 118 people who would be there.

(5) Six people recommitted their lives to Christ, and one made a first-time commitment to Christ.

It was an unbelievable day. God gets all the glory for it. He is absolutely awesome. Thanks to all of you for **praying** for us.

Our vision is to introduce thousands of people to our Lord and Savior. One thing we know for sure – HE PROVIDES. He truly is in the miracle working business. This was surely a GOD THING.

Margaret

FOUR – A NEW CHURCH PROVIDES A PUBLIC PREACHING PLACE (Acts 9:20; 10:42; 14:7; 16:10; 20:20)

Saul, later to become the Apostle Paul, begins his ministry. "At once He began to **preach** in the synagogues that Jesus is the Son of God" (Acts 9:20).

Simon Peter shares the message that Jesus gave the apostles in Acts 1:3, when Jesus talked about the kingdom of God. "He commanded us to **preach** to the people and to testify that He is the one whom God appointed as judge of the living and the dead" (10:42).

"But they found out about it and fled to the Lycaonian cities of Lystra and Derbe and to the surrounding country, where they continued to **preach the good news**" (14:6-7).

"After Paul had seen the vision, we got ready at once to leave for Macedonia, concluding that God had called us to **preach the gospel** to them" (16:10).

Paul gives a ministerial review of his ministry in Ephesus. "You know that I have not hesitated to **preach** anything that would be helpful to you but have taught you publicly and from house to house" (20:20).

Preaching the living Word brings life. Are we the only ones in our local church who should preach and hear the gospel? What about those who never have, or never will, attend our church? They need the gospel preached to them. A new church offers an additional opportunity for them to hear the gospel.

The following statistics from my own fellowship are used solely for illustrative purposes. Since requirements for covenant membership in the Wesleyan Church could be more stringent, making it difficult to compare, I trust you will do your own analyzing within your membership and attendance structure.

Approximately eight percent (8%) of the morning worship attendance statistically disappear from The Wesleyan Church every year.

A covenant member, our highest membership bond, is one who is inside the church in a special relationship. They pledge themselves publicly to the full membership requirements of the church. A covenant member takes membership vows that uniquely require faithful attendance, giving of resources and a holy life. They become, in the best sense of the word, insiders, eligible for church leadership positions and responsibilities. That sketches it in broad strokes.

By the same avenue of accountability, the church body welcomes the new covenant member and assumes a high degree of spiritual responsibility for them and their family. As a member of the church body, when another member suffers or rejoices we experience similar emotions with them. They are a part of the body of Christ, as we are.

What has happened to covenant members in The Wesleyan Church and their effect on the life of the church?

By our record keeping of membership, new covenant members come from conversions and transfers from other denominations, or another Wesleyan Church. Covenant members cease to be members of a local church by death, transfer to another Wesleyan Church, transfer to another denomination, or simply dropped from the rolls due to inactivity. Those dropped from the rolls disappear.

The numbers of covenant members who are dropped or disappear from a Wesleyan local church roll each year dramatically affect attendance and resources. It is not only the former members who are lost to the church, but also those they influence to attend the local church.

Let me illustrate by using a Wesleyan church that averages 100 in morning worship attendance from 1989-1999. They will have 68 covenant members. They will lose slightly more than two percent (1.5 per year) of their covenant members each year over a decade. Thus, in a ten-year period they will lose 15 covenant members who are dropped from the rolls without any official record of where they went.

However, the local church loses more in attendance than just the 15 members. Each member, conservatively, influences the attendance of at least three other people. They may be relatives or friends. When you add the covenant member number together with those they influence, it will approach eight people per year or 80 in a decade. In simple numbers it would look like this:

TYPICAL YEAR IN A WESLEYAN CHURCH

100 - Average attendance	500 - Average attendance
68 - Covenant members	340 - Covenant members
2 - Covenant members dropped	10 - Covenant members dropped
6 - People influenced to leave	30 - Influenced to leave
92 - Remaining at year's end	460 - Remaining at year's end
8 - Total attendance loss	40 - Total attendance loss

The figure of covenant membership dropped each year with the added assumption of their influence on others attending, means the average Wesleyan church loses eight percent of its morning worship attendance each year by people officially being unaccounted for any longer. This was confirmed by statistics from all of our churches in North America from 1989-1999. To further check this observation, I took the statistics of one large church over the same ten-year period. The figures from the large church closely matched those for the whole church.

Where do they go? Is it possible some of them could have been saved for Christ by the planting of a new church in a nearby community? A new church will conserve some of those we lose every year. Instead of asking, "Where did they go?" let us give them an additional church to attend. The more churches we have in an area, the stronger every church in the area will be. In addition, in particular, if it is another church in your fellowship of belief.

FIVE– A NEW CHURCH IS THE MOST EFFECTIVE EVANGELISTIC TOOL (Acts 2:38-39; 14:21)

The first sermon delivered on the grand opening of the church produced this response. "When the people heard this, they were cut to the heart and said to Peter and the other apostles, 'Brothers, what shall we do?' Peter replied, 'Repent and be baptized, every one of you, in the name of Jesus Christ for the **forgiveness of your sins**. And you will receive the gift of the Holy Spirit. The promise is for you and your children, and for all who are far off – for all whom the Lord our God will call'" (Acts 2:37-39).

"They preached the good news in that city [Derbe] and **won** a large number of disciples" (14:21).

A new church cannot properly start without evangelism. Yet, it is possible to evangelize and not plant a new church. Many well-meaning leaders do evangelize, but omit planting new churches, the most effective evangelistic method, from their spiritual arsenal.

The church continues to be God's plan to reach the lost world we live in today. Evangelistic strategies not connected to the planting of new churches fail God's foremost plan.

Various statistics compiled from many sources all come to the same conclusion. New churches do a better job of evangelism than older established churches.

An established church with an average attendance of 100 will have two conversions per year.

A new church with an average attendance of 100 will have eleven conversions per year.

Why? Some reasons exist.

1. They make available additional geographic and cultural points of access into the church.

2. Members of a new church, by a higher percentage, invite more lost acquaintances to church than do believers of established churches.

3. Because we attempt something great for God, like the planting of a new church, a new anointing by the Holy Spirit takes place. He brings a fresh touch of spiritual vitality to both the old and new congregation.

4. Being a part of the new church appeals even to the unsaved. Surveys strongly indicate that people not currently in a church will more likely respond to an invitation to attend a new church than an established one.

5. New churches win more people to Jesus Christ, per member and dollar spent.

6. A new church has added flexibility. The answer, "we've always done it this way," does not carry weight. Only a short past exists.

7. A new church presents a new container for the gospel. People often do not reject the gospel, but they will reject the container coated with unnecessary coverings.

8. A new church can offer a different worship style geared to evangelizing the currently unreached. Established churches will have a worship style that predominantly strengthens and meets the needs of its current members. Nothing is wrong with that arrangement. However, not everyone will like your worship style.

"What is wrong with our worship style?" you ask. "Must we always have something new and different?"

No! We do not always need something new and different. We already have plenty of differences. We do not ordinarily recognize them. Let me share some examples.

When I visit a church, usually the pastor or a leading layperson will confidently inform me of this truth. "Ours is not the typical church." And they are right! It does not exist, except in the figment of the imagination.

Some churches will use choirs only if they are dressed in their Sunday best – no robes. Other churches want their choir to wear robes over their Sunday best garments.

Choirs! Some churches consider choirs as a thing from the past. They only want a worship team up front to lead the worship service.

Some churches sing out of soft cover gospel songbooks that have shaped notes, because they read music by the shape of the note. Others require and use only a formal hymnal. Others do not want a hymnbook or songbook of any kind, only praise choruses, and preferably from a Power Point presentation.

One minister will stand behind a pulpit, while another does not use a pulpit, just a lectern stand, or no stand at all.

In some churches, the thought of having a bulletin with an order of service would be interfering with the work of the Holy Spirit. In others, they believe the Holy Spirit can give inspiration for the order of service before Sunday morning.

Do differences exist? Sure! Services will be conducted every Sunday in Japanese, Chinese, Spanish, Lakota, Northern English, Southern English, Eastern English and Western English.

Does a typical church exist? I think not!

In churches, whether considered blue-collar, middle-class, upper middle-class, first church or second church, I have worshiped and experienced the presence of God in a variety of worship styles. Did all of them suit my personal preferences? No! However, they met a need in their community and culture.

When the pastor faithfully preaches the Bible from the pulpit, and the Bible is faithfully taught in a class setting, all of the other surrounding styles may vary as long as they lead people to Jesus Christ.

In North America, millions of people do not know Jesus Christ as their personal Savior and Lord. We definitely need numerous new churches to evangelize more effectively our local mission field.

When the church gets to heaven it will do everything better, except for one thing. In heaven, it will sing better, preach better, laugh better, praise better, celebrate better, rejoice better and many other things better. The one thing it cannot do better, or do at all in heaven, is evangelize the lost.

SIX – A NEW CHURCH TEACHES THE BIBLE
(Acts 4:2; 5:19-21; 5:42; 8:4; 11:25-26; 18:11; 20:20; 28:31)

Peter and John's teaching upset the Jewish religious leaders. "They were greatly disturbed because the apostles were **teaching** the people and proclaiming in Jesus the resurrection of the dead" (Acts 4:2).

"But during the night an angel of the Lord opened the doors of the jail and brought them out. 'Go, stand in the temple courts,' he said, 'and tell the people the full message of this new life.' At daybreak they entered the temple courts, as they had been told, and began **to teach** the people" (Acts 5:19-21).

The early church in Jerusalem taught the good news from the beginning of its existence. "Day after day, in the temple courts and from house to house, they never stopped **teaching** and proclaiming the good news that Jesus is the Christ" (Acts 5:42).

The principle of team teaching is found in Acts 11:25-26. "Then Barnabas went to Tarsus to look for Saul, and when he found him, he brought him to Antioch. So for a whole year Barnabas and Saul met with the church and **taught** great numbers of people. The disciples were called Christians first at Antioch."

The Corinthian church benefited from Paul's teaching ministry. "So Paul stayed a whole year and a half, **teaching** them the word of God" (Acts 18:11).

Paul's farewell message to the Ephesian church contained this statement: "You know that I have not hesitated to preach anything that would be helpful to you but have **taught you** publicly and from house to house" (Acts 20:20).

The last verse in the Book of Acts records Paul's ministry in Rome, "Boldly and without hindrance he preached the kingdom of God and **taught** about the Lord Jesus Christ" (Acts 28:31).

New churches can begin with a fanfare not primarily based on the preaching and teaching of the Bible. Music and worship styles can attract those desiring something different. In addition, these have a prominent place in outreach and discipleship.

However, the solid spiritual health of any church body resides in its membership being rooted and grounded in the faith. No other material or method can replace preaching and teaching the Bible. God has no second book equal to the Bible for communicating faith and doctrines.

Sunday school or church school continues to be a main small group ministry for the spiritual development of everyone in the church. Other small group ministries may be used to start a new church, or provide ministry in an established church. However, studies and statistics reveal that the core of small group discipleship ministry continues to be the Sunday school. The organized balanced study of the Bible through the Sunday school develops disciples. Through the study of the Bible and fellowship with others, people grow stronger in the Lord. Without the Sunday school, the disciple-making process of a new or established church will be stunted and fall short of its responsibility.

If we ignore the Sunday school and its benefits for discipleship, we lose. The importance of this aspect of church life cannot be over emphasized. We need the Sunday school active and alive in every church. We should be alarmed for the discipleship ministry of our church when we allow the Sunday school to be ignored.

While this discourse is concerned for the most part with new church planting, an established church will be hindered in developing leaders for new churches without an active Sunday school ministry. Numerous churches exist today because they started as Sunday school classes in a community. A renewed emphasis on the Sunday school in established churches will enhance the church planting effort.

Preoccupied with doing ministry ourselves, we may forget to train others to do it. When trained, disciples must be released for expanded ministry. Our tendency, too often, is to protect and hold on to people, rather than free them.

Ultimately the goal is for those evangelized to become disciples in the church.

To illustrate the differences and yet the connection between evangelism and discipleship observe the following:

> In evangelism, the issue of salvation
> In discipleship, the interactions
>
> In evangelism, the Gospel informs
> In discipleship, the Gospel is imaged
>
> In evangelism, inspiration
> In discipleship, involvement
>
> In evangelism, Christ
> In discipleship, Christ and the Church

Teaching the Bible in a Sunday school or small group setting will evangelize the lost and provide discipleship training for the converted. The next logical step out of this wholesome spiritual environment will be new church planting.

SEVEN – A NEW CHURCH OFFERS ANOTHER PLACE FOR CHRISTIAN SERVICE (Acts 6:3; 9:36; 11:25-26; 11:29-30; 17:15)

"Brothers, choose seven men from among you who are known to be full of the Spirit and wisdom. We will turn this **responsibility over to them** and will give our attention to prayer and the ministry of the word" (Acts 6:3-4).

"In Joppa there was a disciple named Tabitha (which, when translated, is Dorcas), who was **always doing good** and helping the poor" (Acts 9:36).

"Then Barnabas went to Tarsus to look for Saul, and when he found him, he brought him to Antioch. So for a whole year **Barnabas and Saul met with the church** and taught a great number of people. The disciples were called Christians first at Antioch" (Acts 11:25-26).

"The disciples, each according to his ability, decided to provide help for the brothers living in Judea. This they did, sending their gift to the elders **by Barnabas and Saul**" (Acts 11:29-30).

"The brothers immediately sent Paul to the coast, but **Silas and Timothy stayed at Berea**. The men who **escorted** Paul brought him to Athens and then left with instructions for Silas and Timothy to join him as soon as possible" (Acts 17:14-15).

Prominent characters in the Book of Acts like Simon Peter and Paul can cause us to overlook the other people who served in the early church bodies. Would the church have been as successful without James (the brother of Jesus),

42

Barnabas, Silas, Timothy, Luke, Stephen, Philip, Procorus, Nicanor, Timon, Parmenas, Nicolas, Cornelius, Mark, Titius Justus, Apollos, Priscilla, Aquila, Sopater, Aristarchus, Secundus, Gaius, Tychicus, Trophimus, Ephesian elders and Agabus?

While leadership figures like Simon Peter and Paul stand out, would there be leaders without others following them and providing different levels of leadership?

In the church of Jesus Christ, everyone has a place of service. Everyone is needed. Places of service may be more recognized in some areas than others. As an example, I strongly believe that the person(s) who keep a nursery so young parents can attend worship service are equally important with the minister preaching in the pulpit. Their places of service compliment each other. Whatever our place of God-called service in the church, it is equally as valuable as any other person's place of service in God's eyes. Moreover, it should be in our eyes as well.

A new church opens up a new dimension of service for those involved. At the beginning, everyone has to fill several roles. Tasks that need to be done often call for a stretching of personal gifts until others more able can take our place. People in a new church quickly find places of Christian service in the church and involvement in ministry outreach. They may be involved in setting up chairs, sound equipment and the nursery. During the same period, the same person may also be part of the worship service and teach a Sunday school class.

When a mother church sends out some of its leaders to start a new church, it hurts to lose leadership, stability and friendships. However, it soon discovers that some members, who have been sitting on the sidelines of leadership, waiting and willing to serve, fill the leadership void. The convenience and the comfort of an established church can be a hindrance in developing leaders. Stretch yourself spiritually.

EIGHT – A NEW CHURCH TRAINS LAY LEADERS TO BECOME PREACHERS (Acts 6:10; 14:23)

"These men began to argue with Stephen, but they could not stand up against the wisdom or the Spirit by whom **he spoke**" (Acts 6:9b-10).

"Paul and Barnabas **appointed elders for them in each church** and, with prayer and fasting, committed them to the Lord, in whom they had put their trust" (Acts 14:23).

John Wesley, in his earlier ministry days, resisted lay people as ministerial leaders. However, God kept sending and using lay people to preach and teach and move the church forward. John Wesley reluctantly realized that God uses lay people for ministry and in ministry roles. They could minister first and then be trained as they served.

We have gotten too far away from our early beginnings when many churches came into existence through the leadership of lay ministers. Do we restrict ourselves when we hinder ministry until training is complete? I think we slow lay ministers down unnecessarily when they are experienced, gifted, and people follow them.

An essential element for the church to be a dynamic movement led by the Holy Spirit is lay ministry. When we show enthusiasm for their work and approve, allow, encourage and train lay people to be active in the ministry of planting new churches, we will build God's kingdom on earth more rapidly. Lay ministry was an integral part of our heritage and needs to be more active in our future.

44

Pastor Chris Conrad planted a church in Spearfish, South Dakota, in 1993. Spearfish is a small town located between Rapid City, South Dakota and Gillette, Wyoming. The church developed until it averaged 291 in morning worship attendance in1999. Pastor Conrad then accepted a call in January 2000 to plant a church in Wisconsin. He prepared the church for his leaving by training his successor. The following wonderful example of training lay leaders to become preachers is retold in Pastor Conrad's own words:

I first met Mark and Christina Fuhr almost three years ago. Before long, I got together with them, to hear more about their background. It was then that I learned a bit more of their background. Mark opened up his heart to a relationship with Jesus Christ while he and Christina were dating in college.

After going into the Air Force, Mark graduated first in his class in Officer's Training School. He became an Air Force pilot and had a good career in the service.

Since getting out, Mark's dream of being an airline pilot never fully materialized. One of the most discouraging events in Mark's life occurred when he was hired by Continental Airlines one day, only to have the company file Chapter 11 the next, ending his 24 hour career with the company. Although this greatly frustrated and mystified Mark, it now seems obvious that God was shutting a door to a career that would have been natural and easy for Mark . . . but was not God's BEST for him.

After being involved in a company that built and sold planes, he had gone to work as an insurance adjuster, which is what he was doing when he moved to Spearfish.

It wasn't long before I encouraged them both to attend our Spiritual Gift's Class. As it turned out, they both had the spiritual gift of leadership, and he had the spiritual gift of teaching.

After a few subsequent conversations with Mark, it was clear to me that he had the potential of being a great pastor. I began to give him and Christina ministry opportunities where they could get their feet wet and build credibility with our young congregation.

Because their passion was small groups, I allowed them to head up this ministry. I also took time to help Mark develop his teaching gift. Soon, whenever I was out of town, I allowed Mark to speak in my absence. These positions allowed them to quickly become well respected throughout the church.

I then began to vision-cast with Mark about coming on staff. Although the job definitely interested him, he was deeply skeptical about making the leap for a few different reasons:

He didn't have any "formal" training as a pastor. It would mean an adjustment in their lifestyle.

After a few months of wrestling with the Holy Spirit on this issue, Mark and Christina came to the conclusion that coming on staff was indeed the Lord's will. In October 1999, the Lord helped us raise the funds for their salary, and they came on staff.

Four months later, I left Countryside in Mark's hands, to pursue God's call on my life in Madison, Wisconsin. The board and the District Superintendent, Isaac Smith, both felt comfortable in Mark's ability to lead the church effectively during the transition period. Recently though, the board affirmed God's call on Mark's life to lead Countryside for a longer period of time and they are no longer searching for a Senior Pastor.

Mark's story gives me great joy when I see what he allowed the Holy Spirit to do in his life. Here's a guy who started out gun shy about any church involvement who is now pastoring the church. One of the greatest privileges of leadership is to encourage people like Mark and Christina to experience the full potential God has placed inside of them, even if that means a major career change. God has blessed them because of their obedience and is using them to change lives!

It is my firm conviction that if we are going to see church plants flourish in number, like we need to, then we must release ministry to capable lay people who are called by God to lead churches.

All of us in ministry face challenges to make a movement happen. One of them is a lack of trained ministers to fill current pulpits and expected new churches. That means that current lay people in our churches are a vital spiritual element in having a major move forward for the kingdom of God. Without current lay people accepting the call to be church planters, it will not happen.

Lay people in a community, already established with jobs, and understanding the local culture, can become bi-vocational pastors. Other lay people can advance the kingdom by accepting God's call on their life for full time ministry. We as a church need a major shift in our thinking. We must allow lay people to become ministers. Train them as soon as possible, but do not slow down their ministry when God calls.

NINE - A NEW CHURCH CROSSES CULTURAL BARRIERS (Acts 8:34-35; 10:1-47; 16:9; 22:21)

"The **eunuch [an Ethiopian]** asked Philip, 'Tell me, please, who is the prophet talking about, himself or someone else?' Then Philip began with that very passage of Scripture and told him the good news about Jesus" (Acts 8:34-35).

Acts chapter ten introduces us to **Cornelius, a Roman centurion,** who finds Christ through the ministry of Simon Peter, a Jew. Cornelius' conversion compelled the early church, though reluctant at first, to recognize that the good news about Jesus Christ belonged to everyone.

"During the night Paul had a vision of a man in Macedonia standing and begging him, 'Come over to Macedonia and help us'" (Acts 16:9). This man later turned out to be the **Philippian jailer** (Acts 16:27-34).

Paul speaking before a hostile mob in Jerusalem gave his testimony. When he said at the end of it, "Then the Lord said to me, 'Go; I will send you far away to the **Gentiles**'" (Acts 22:21), the crowd erupted with anger and called for his death.

Our commission includes looking to saturate geographic (Acts 1:8), linguistic (Acts 2:5-7) and cross-cultural (Acts chapter 10) groups. The way to do it is by planting new churches to cross those barriers. Everyone, EVERYONE, every one needs the gospel!

A wonderful privilege and joy is to visit, work with and serve people of many cultures. Every culture has something spiritually unique to offer to others.

Several years ago, a new church plant in Central Canada started with the intention of reaching Anglo-Saxons with the gospel. The pastor soon discovered a number of different cultures lived in the community and surrounding area. The plans changed and he set about to plant a multi-cultural church.

Different events throughout the year highlighted their diversity, yet unity in Christ. Activities featured one cultural group a month. The highlighted cultural group presented music, fellowship times and food, leading to a better understanding of other heritages. What a thrill I personally experienced when I saw the choir reflect the beauty of the rainbow as different cultures joined in praise.

A new church in Kansas City started in 1999 with a vision for primarily reaching African-American people in their target area. After nine months of existence, the new church had an average attendance of 100 on Sunday morning. However, it was a congregation of varied cultures. A slight majority might have composed the original design of the church, but pastor and people had adapted to meet the needs of the community. And, that means everyone is welcome. The experience of worshiping with them is something I will long remember as the people sang and shared, and the pastor fervently preached the Word of God.

A new church can definitely cross cultural barriers.

TEN – A NEW CHURCH MENTORS NEW BELIEVERS
(Acts 9:26-27; 20:20; 20:31, 36; 20:34-36; 20:27)

Thank God for Barnabas who mentored the apostle Paul. "When he [Saul] came to Jerusalem, he tried to join the disciples, but they were all afraid of him, not believing that he really was a disciple. **But Barnabas took him** and brought him to the apostles. He told them how Saul on his journey had seen the Lord and that the Lord had spoken to him, and how in Damascus he had preached fearlessly in the name of Jesus" (Acts 9:26-27).

One of several mentors who influenced my life is Dr. Marling Elliott, a retired professor of Southern Wesleyan University. His teaching style resonated with my wanting to learn in my formative years of ministry. He taught the Book of Acts. From the way he presented the book, even today when you name a chapter I immediately see the settings in my mind. The reason – my mentor Dr. Elliott taught me. In the classroom and outside of it he mentored the Christian life. Later in my ministry, I had the privilege to serve as his pastor for six years. We remain life long friends.

When influencers give their lives to Christ and mentor others, the kingdom moves forward. Paul described part of his ministry of teaching and preaching as what was "helpful" (Acts 20:20). Paul the model church planter exhibited a high work ethic as he went "publicly and from house to house," "night and day," and "hard work" (Acts 20:20, 31, 35). It takes more than looking busy and acting important to get the job done for the Lord.

Every group of people includes some that will influence others. They believe and express confidence in the potential that they see in another individual. Moreover, because of their own influence, they help others decide to trust their judgment. Paul lived a holy life before them as part of the mentoring process (Acts 20:33-34). His personal motives or financial transactions were beyond reproach when closely examined.

The Apostle Paul emptied his emotions (Acts 20:31, 36), into his mentoring work. They cried together. They developed a strong bond of love and appreciation. Mentoring out of an environment of love for each other and for kingdom work can make church planting a movement for Christ.

In the mentoring activities of Paul, he modeled the joy and privilege of giving. A church planting movement that wants to be progressive must teach and model giving as Paul did (Acts 20:35).

In Acts 20:27 to the Ephesian elders Paul stated, "For I have not hesitated to proclaim to you the whole will of God." That is mentoring.

Did Paul do what he said he did? He preached. He taught. He mentored. He released them for ministry and, in particular, church planting. Note the following list of people Paul mentored and released for ministry. Also, observe that some of them planted churches.

Apollos in Ephesus (Acts 18:24)
Epaphras in Colosse (Col. 1:7)
Erastus in Macedonia (Acts 19:22)
Epaphroditus in Phillipi (Phil. 2:25)
Gaius in Derbe (Acts 20:4)
Gaius and Aristatchus in Ephesus (Acts 19:29)
Priscilla and Aquila in Ephesus (Acts 18:19)
Secundus in Thessalonica (Acts 20:4)

Sopater in Berea (Acts 20:4)
Timothy in Macedonia (Acts 19:22)
Titus in Crete (Titus 1:5)
Trophimus in Province of Asia (Acts 20:4)

Establish a church and almost immediately a mentoring process begins. That process then continues for the life of the new church, hopefully for at least a hundred years into the future.

I met Al and Pam Goracke recently. Their story illustrates the value of mentoring.

Al owned a family dry cleaning business. Al and his wife Pam were very successful in business, with four stores scattered throughout the city, but without God and a church in their lives. You meet Al and his energy connects with you immediately. Al is a leader by all definitions of the word.

About five years ago, while Al was driving on the job, he heard a sermon by a well-known radio minister, that the Lord used to convict him. Al pulled to the side of the road and prayed the sinner's prayer. The Lord saved Al and soon Pam joined him as a Christian.

They started attending a church in Blaine, Minnesota. Their pastor began a mentoring process with the young Christian businessman. For the past several years, Al Goracke has served as an assistant pastor while still operating his business. This year, after their pastor resigned to accept another position, the church called Al as their pastor.

Preparing for fulltime ministry, he and his wife are selling their business.

Al and Pam intend to plant a church in the near future, either as founding pastors, or leading their church to mother a new church.

Mentoring takes time. However, the amount of time can vary from a few moments each week to an hour or more.

How rewarding it is to be told how much our help and example meant at a crucial time in a person's life. Often, we were not consciously aware of being a mentor at the time. One thought to constantly remember; we mentor all the time. We have an impact on everyone we meet. As others observe our lives, we cannot help but influence them. The question I ask myself and trust you will as well is "Am I a good or bad mentor?"

ELEVEN – A NEW CHURCH SUPPORTS WORLDWIDE MISSION ACTIVITY (Acts 13:2-3; 16:9-10)

"While they were worshiping the Lord and fasting, the Holy Spirit said, '**Set apart for me Barnabas and Saul** for the work to which I called them.' So after they had fasted and prayed, they placed their hands on them and sent them off" (Acts 13:2-3).

"During the night **Paul had a vision** of a man of Macedonia standing and begging him, 'Come over to Macedonia and help us'" (Acts 16:9).

New churches provide another place to provide a stimulus for worldwide mission activity. They offer another house of worship where a mission message can be shared. Prayer and financial support can be encouraged. Eventually, people will go to the mission fields from new churches.

Sometimes the impression can be given that an unhealthy tension exists between "the ends of the earth" (Acts 1:8) and the needs at Jerusalem, Judea and Samaria. The home base provides support for the overseas mission outreach. The more healthy churches we start at home, the more we will fulfill the total picture of Acts 1:8. Both need our prayers and financial support.

One of the exciting developments being observed by this office is a new church beginning to be involved in missionary activity. The new church begins to be a sharer of resources rather than being solely dependent on others. This support is more than just finances. It is also future personnel for overseas ministries. Both home and overseas missions have an important place of interdependence and cooperative effort. A larger home base enables them to do more.

Giving to missions honors God. He in turn honors the local church with a mission mindset. Most every minister can relate unusual stories about their first pastorate. I am no exception.

My first pastorate helped mold my ministry. The congregation and their leadership endured many things and followed my leadership when things did not look very good for the future of the church. I love those people and their faith.

When I arrived, I discovered the treasury was "broke", parsonage payments were pressing, and we had some past due bills that needed addressing. At the first church board meeting, I proposed we start giving ten percent of our income each month to mission causes outside of our own church. They agreed in a blind, impossible act of faith.

At the end of the year, finances had tripled, attendance had doubled, bills were current and we had paid our denominational assessment 100%. I attribute it to prayer, the faithfulness of the people and God's Holy Spirit bringing revival. A major part of the recovery process for the church revolved around our giving to missions. Struggling churches should check their involvement in missions. Trusting God increases faith, not failure.

TWELVE – A HEALTHY NEW CHURCH STARTS OTHER CHURCHES (Acts 13:2-3; 16:9)

"While they were worshiping the Lord and fasting, the Holy Spirit said, 'Set apart for me Barnabas and Saul for the work to which I have called them.' So after they had fasted and prayed, they placed their hands on them and sent them off" (Acts 13:2-3).

The rationale for more churches is that every person in an area will have an opportunity to hear and know the gospel, and receive or reject Jesus Christ as their personal Savior through the witness of a reproducing church. God's number one chosen instrument to proclaim the good news continues to be the church. God's plan to reach the world continues through His church.

Note the spread of the good news through new churches in the Book of Acts.

How many places can we suggest new churches were started from the Jerusalem and Antioch churches and listed in the Book of Acts according to the context and later references?

Chapter

1   Jerusalem

2   Parthians (Iran), Elamites (east of Tigris and Euphrates Rivers), Mesopotamia (Babylon), Judea, Cappadocia (area north of Tarsus), Pontus (Turkey today), Asia (cities of Ephesus,

Smyrna and Pergamos), Phrygia (mountain area of Turkey), Pamphyllia (south Turkey), Egypt, Libya near Cyrene (north cost of Africa in modern Libya), Rome, Cretans (isle of Crete), and Arabs (between the Red Sea and the Persian Gulf)

4	Cypress
6	Greece, Antioch
8	Judea, Samaria, Ethiopia, Samaritan towns
9	Damascus, Tarsus, Lydda, Sharon
10	Caesarea
11	Phoenicia (near Tyre), Cyprus, Antioch, Tarsus, Cyrene
13	Salamis (in Cypress), Paphos (in Cypress), Perga, Pisidian Antioch
14	Iconium, Lystra, Derbe
15	Cypress, Syria, Cilicia
16	Derbe, Lystra, Iconium, Phrygia, Galatia (center of Asia Minor), Philippi, Thyatira
17	Thessalonica, Berea, Athens
18	Corinth, Pontus, Ephesus, Achaia (Greece), Galatia, Phygia, Ephesus
19	Ephesus, Macedonia (Philippi)
20	Macedonia, Greece, Berea, Thessalonica, Derbe, province of Asia, Troas, Miletus
21	Tyre, Ptolemais, Caesarea, Cyprus
27	Thessalonia, Sidon
28	Puteoli (port in Italy), Bay of Naples, Rome

The Apostle Paul, the leader of the early church planting movement, planted many churches as a direct result of Pentecost. Most of the churches he started had their roots in the Day of Pentecost when some of the people from those cities and areas were present.

This reminds us, once again, that when the Holy Spirit inspires us to plant a church or churches in a city or an area, He prepares the spiritual soil ahead of time.

At a recent church planter's conference attended by approximately 100 couples, all of whom had planted a church in recent years, I had the privilege to be inspired by these men and women. Their dynamic, frontline, innovative leadership charged the air. Being with these high-energy persons with big visions for God increased my vision.

Two different church planters and their spouses during the conference said they wanted to have an hour to talk with me about plans for planting churches in their area. I arranged to meet one couple for lunch and the other at 3:00 p.m. in a lobby area.

Rev. Wayne Otto and his wife pioneered a church in Greenville, Michigan in 1994 after serving on the staff of a large church in Indiana. The Lord has blessed their efforts with phenomenal growth through reaching the unchurched and leading them to a saving knowledge of Jesus Christ. Their church grew in five years until it reached over 500 in worship attendance. They met me for lunch. Then they shared their vision. What a vision!

They plan to mother a new church every year for the next fourteen years by providing people and financial resources. They currently have people attending their church in Greenville from Gratton, Belding, Ionia, Stanton, Crystal, Carson City, Edmore, Ithaca, Howard City, Lakeview, Big Rapids, Cedar Springs, Kent City and Sparta communities. These communities surround Greenville. Built into the church mothering process they expect each new church will plant another church by its fifth birthday. The first one has already been planted.

Meeting with the Otto family for lunch gave me my first major surprise of the day with the enormity of their vision for new church planting.

I met with the Rev. Raymond Smith and his spouse at 3:00 p.m. The Smith family planted their church two years ago. The church is nearing 100 in attendance. They shared a vision called the *Harvest Cell Church Network*.

Interesting! Their vision for new church planting had their new church mothering thirteen new churches in a few years. To the north from their church, they plan to plant churches in Barrie, Stroud and Orlillia. On the east side, they have targeted the cities of Holland Landing, Sharon and Queensville. South of the mother church, they will concentrate on Newmarket, Aurora and Oak Ridge. West of the Harvest Church, they intend to plant churches in Beeton, Alliston, Tottenham and Cookstown. Their theme, *"Without Faith it is Impossible to Please God."*

They defined their mission. *The mission of the Harvest Cell Church Network is to birth and administrate an aggressive interconnected network made up of dozens of church planting cell churches.*

They believe that church planting is NOT dependent upon:

      (1) Money
      (2) Ordained clergy
      (3) Buildings
      (4) Physical resources

They believe that church planting is ALL about:

      (1) New Testament community
      (2) Equipping the saints
      (3) Lay-led ministry
      (4) Five fold ministry

I believe their vision for even greater things for the Lord's work should motivate all of us to do something. These two parsonage families daily live out the Great Commission. How about you and your church?

A local church that mothers another church provides some essential elements more efficiently than even a district or the general church. Those elements often include a core group, ministry resources, finances, prayer and most importantly, emotional support. Their knowledge of the area enables the new church to better target its area for unreached people.

NEW CHURCHES BEGIN IN A NUMBER OF SETTINGS

A. School building
B. Home
C. Community or apartment clubhouse
D. Vacant mall space
E. Churches that regularly meet on Saturday
F. Hotel conference room
G. Funeral home chapel
H. Restaurant dining room
I. Vacant church building
J. Large mobile home
K. Theater
L. Tent – according to location
M. You name it

PRINCIPLES UNDERGIRDING
NEW CHURCH PLANTING

Twelve reasons have been shared for starting a new church in the Book of Acts. Those reasons for existence also apply to an established church. Every pastor and his congregation can do a spiritual reality check with the twelve reasons for starting a church and see if they continue in these things.

Undergirding the reasons for a new church are seven principles for new church planting.

1.   **Prayer and Fasting** – Acts 1:14; 2:42; 4:24; 6:4; 10:9; 10:31; 13:2; 14:23; 16:16; 21:5; 28:8.

Church planters must solicit prayer partners and communicate with them regularly. District leaders will often request new church planters to recruit 120 Upper Room Prayer Partners.

2.   **Holy Spirit's Leadership** - Acts 1:2, 5, 7, 16; 2:4, 33, 38; 4:8, 25, 31; 5:3, 32; 6:5; 7:51, 55; 8:15, 16, 17, 19; 9:17, 31; 10:38, 44, 45, 47; 11:15, 16, 24; 13:2-4, 9, 52; 15:8, 28; 16:6; 19:2, 6; 20:23, 28; 21:11; 28:25.

Jesus Christ promised that the Holy Spirit would lead and guide us (John 16:12-13). That promise He fulfilled in the Book of Acts 2:1-14, and in the church today. The Holy Spirit's presence must be with us or we try in vain.

3.   **God Called Leaders** – Acts 1:8; 5:9; 6:3; 8:35; 9:15; 13:2-3; 18:19; 18:27.

Others ask, "What do you look for in church planters? What characteristics must be there?

First, the planters must have a clear call from God to plant a new church. That call will strengthen them when difficult days come, as they will. The call provides spiritual stability in their relationship to God's purpose for their lives.

First, (this is a second first) their spouses need to be supportive in every way possible.

First, (this is a third first) in their relationship with others, they genuinely need to have a love for people and their spiritual condition. People instinctively know whether your expressed Christian love is real. Christian love for others cannot be faked. It has to be real, unconditional love for church planters to reach people for Christ.

Second, as church planters relate to others, they have to have leadership abilities that work with people or others will not follow them. That leadership has to be exhibited while harnessed to work with other people. A domineering style of leadership without careful consideration for others will lead to failure. At best, leaders who are too dominant will not last very long in a church-planting situation. Their extreme dominance will express itself in not being willing to let others participate in the leadership of the church.

Check the scripture references in the Book of Acts. You will discover strong leaders working effectively with people.

4.   **A God Given Vision** – Acts 13:2-3; 16:9

In the previous section, we observed that church planters need a definite call from God. In addition to the call, the Lord gives a vision for the place of service.

The Holy Spirit brings to a prospective church planter a place in general like Macedonia (Acts 16:9). At that time, Paul did not know the place in particular would be in a jail and subsequently in a jailer's house. I believe the jailer was the man in the Macedonian vision.

Our general order in fulfilling a vision for a new church in a community contains most if not all elements in this order.

    a.   The church planter receives a vision for a particular area in general.

    b.   We do demographics of the area.

      c.   The church planters are matched with an area specifically that matches their background, training and calling.

      d.   The church planter arrives and begins to fulfill the vision.

A personal vision will challenge and consume us. It is worth the cost.

5.   **Preaching and Teaching the Word** - Acts 4:31; 6:2, 4, 7; 8:4, 14, 25; 11:1; 12:24; 13:5, 7, 44, 46, 48, 49; 14:25; 15:35, 36; 16:6, 32; 17:13; 18:11; 19:10, 20; 20:32.

The authority of the Bible for directing life continues to be challenged. Reasons for rejection of its authority include irrelevancy, distortions, dated, full of inconsistencies and definitely not God's Word. At best, its detractors acknowledge it as a book with some truth, but not the whole truth.

     A basic principle of new church planting continues to be the preaching and teaching of the Bible. It is relevant and timeless in at least five dimensions.

     a. The day it was written

     b. Yesterdays

     c. Today

     d. Tomorrows

     e. Eternity

6.   **Go to all Cultures with the Gospel** – Acts 8:35; 10:1-47; 11:19-21; 13:2-3; 14:21; 16:9-10; 17:1-34; 18:1-28

In Acts chapter two, the people present at Pentecost came from the present day countries of Albania, parts of Asia, Cyprus, Egypt, Greece, Iran, Iraq, Israel, Italy, Jordan, Lebanon, Libya, Malta, Saudi Arabia, Syria and Turkey. The Holy Spirit came that day to a multiethnic multitude. The gospel touched the then known world.

     In North America, we have the same multi-cultural opportunities to share the gospel. Current immigration trends transform us from a primarily European heritage to an area with cross-cultural bonds to every race and region on the planet. We must respond with new churches.

7.   **Share Responsibilities** – Acts 6:3

The early church started with a spiritual energy in Acts chapter two. The new church in Jerusalem soon met a call for service and outreach beyond the grasp or capabilities of the original apostles. They needed help. They had to delegate and share responsibilities. When they did, the church moved forward.

After observing a number of new church plants over the years, one characteristic has to prevail eventually or the new church will falter and miss its original vision. That trait of sharing leadership, after the initial thrust, has to come forth or the church will soon wither. Moreover, the sooner leadership is shared, the better.

APPENDIX

Starting new churches is not a popular program with some people.

An obvious reason for starting new churches is to take the gospel wherever people live. A larger number of new churches make it possible to reach the maximum number of people.

We need to push our comfort zone.

Not everyone is convinced that starting new churches works. Their local church came into being by some miraculous, unexplained way without it ever being new at one time in history.

SOME MISTAKEN BUT WELL-INTENDED THOUGHTS ABOUT NEW CHURCH PLANTING BY OBJECTORS

One concern by objectors – "Planting new churches means we will ignore our present churches, who need new spiritual life."

Answer – We do want all of our churches to grow. Presently, more than 50% of the resources entrusted to this department are used for existing churches through materials, books and programs. It is not an issue of existing churches or new churches. Ongoing spiritual life and vitality involves both the existing and new churches. New churches in a decade, from experience, will account for more than one-half of the conversion, membership, attendance and financial growth of a denomination.

Another concern by objectors - "A new church close by will hinder our church."

Answer – Some changes may occur in an established church when another church comes into existence close by, but they are not long term changes. I will share one example out of many. Pastor Kinnan's church mothered a new church in Sioux Falls, South Dakota. They joyfully released over 100 people to start the new church. Within a few weeks, they returned to their original attendance. Bill Sullivan, Director of the Church Growth Division of the Church of the Nazarene, calls it *The Miracle of Replenishment.*

When congregations share their most valuable resource, people, they almost always grow to where they started, and even beyond.

Denominational studies show that when other churches of the same denomination are located close to each other in a geographical area, it strengthens every church. The basic truth (assuming you have an active church) - the more churches of your denomination in your area, the stronger will be your church.

Another concern by objectors to new church planting – "Very few new churches survive; why waste the money and the energy to try?"

Answer – This assumption that most new churches fail to survive is only that - an assumption. When denominations through their structures require screening, assessment, and boot camp for church planters, the rate of success has been as high as 92%. If a denomination fails to start new churches, it will slowly fade into oblivion. New churches strive and thrive, when properly started and mentored.

Another objection – "We already have enough little churches. Why not merge some of them and make larger churches instead of planting new ones."

Answer – Small churches, however you define what you mean by small, are a fact of life. Being small in numerical size does not mean being small in ministry. I remember one small community of about thirty people in Nebraska, fifteen miles from the next community. On a high day they will have fifteen present. However, ministers, missionaries and other Christian workers have gone forth from this church over the years. Small in number—it was yet large in influence for God's kingdom.

Do you know the law of merger when two small congregations come together? It is this (and of course someone knows the exception that happened somewhere). When you join two small churches together, within five years the newly formed congregation will be smaller than the once larger of the former two churches. To further illustrate: If you join a fifty and a forty together, in five years you will have just one church that averages less than fifty.

Objection – "We need to concentrate on evangelism. When we do, new churches will probably follow."

Answer – This objection sounds good, but misses a vital, urgent point. New church growth is tied to evangelism. When new churches begin, the overall evangelism effort intensifies. New church planting has been and continues to be, since Christ came, the number one methodology for evangelism.

A big objection – "We cannot afford to start new churches. They cost too much!"

Answer – Actually, we cannot afford not to start new churches. Every year we must start new churches or a day will arrive when we cease to exist. New churches, started the right way, soon become self-supporting, usually within eighteen to twenty-four months. Eventually, they generate income rather than remove it.

A final observation by an objector – "We will mother a new church when the time is right. When we reach this number in attendance, pay off our mortgage and become stronger, we will mother a church."

Answer - It will never happen. What is the right time? When will your church have no financial problems? When will everything be just right? Probably never is the answer. God wants us to move forward – now!

CONCLUSION

The need, the process, the urgency, the building of God's kingdom through new church planting comes into conflict with some current thinking in the church. A battle rages for the minds and hearts of people. Only the Holy Spirit can come and change people's minds and hearts to building His kingdom this way. The Holy Spirit comes when we pray. Bob Logan, noted church planting authority said, "Prayer is not just preparation for the battle, prayer is the battle."

In closing, I would ask you to consider the **ABCDs of CHURCH PLANTING.**

A -   **Ask** in prayer what the Lord would have you do for building His kingdom through new church planting. Can you ignore this number one method of evangelism?

B -   **Believe** it is possible. If where we serve is to be transformed for the better building of God's kingdom, it always begins with us. We must change the way we think.

C -   **Commit** yourself as an individual and as part of the church to do your best. Then go the next step and surrender to God's will and way.

D -   **Determine** that nothing will stop you from doing His will in the matter of new church planting. Stand spiritually tall with a strength that conquers in the name of Jesus Christ.

THE MOST EFFECTIVE METHOD OF EVANGELISM IS NEW CHURCH PLANTING

The church you attend, how did it happen to come into being? In the past, a pastor or a lay person got a burden for a new church and your church came into existence through prayer and sacrifice. May God lay a similar burden on your heart today.

IT IS TIME FOR THE CHURCH TO LIVE IN ACTS CHAPTER TWENTY-NINE

AVAILABLE RESOURCES
FOR CHURCH PLANTING

Dorsey, Jim. *Starter Kit for Starting Strong New Churches: Ideas for Church Start Leaders.* Kansas City: New Start, 1997.

Faircloth, Samuel D. *Church Planting for Reproduction.* Grand Rapids: Baker Book House, 1991.

Feeney, James H. *Church Planting by the Team Method.* Anchorage: Abbott Loop Christian Center, 1988.

Logan, Robert E. and Steven L. Ogne. *Churches Planting Churches.* Carol Stream, IL: ChurchSmart Resources, 1995.

_____. *The Church Planter's Toolkit.* Carol Stream, IL: ChurchSmart Resources, 1991. An audiocassette album.

Malphurs, Aubrey. *Planting Growing Churches for the 21st Century.* Grand Rapids: Baker Book House, 1992.

Mannoia, Kevin W. *Church Planting: The Next Generation.* Indianapolis: Light and Life Press, 1994.

Owen, Roy W., ed. *The Pastor's Helper for Growing a New Church.* New Church Growth Department, Home Mission Board, Southern Baptist Convention.

Schaller, Lyle E. *44 Questions for Church Planters.* Nashville: Abingdon Press, 1991.

Schwarz, Christian A. *Natural Church Development.* Carol Stream, IL: ChurchSmart Resources, 1996.

Sullivan, Bill M. *Starting Strong New Churches.* Kansas City: New Start, 1997.

Tidsworth, Floyd Jr. *Life Cycle of a New Congregation.* Nashville: Broadman Press, 1992.

Wagner, C. Peter. *Church Planting for a Great Harvest.* Ventura, CA: Regal Books, 1990.

Warren, Rick. *The Purpose Driven Church: Growth Without Compromising Your Message and Mission.* Grand Rapids: Zondervan Publishing House, 1995.

CPSIA information can be obtained at www.ICGtesting.com
Printed in the USA
LVOW082032050412

276265LV00004B/4/P